The Book of

FRIENDSHIP

OTHER BOOKS BY CYNDI HAYNES

The Book of Change

2,002 Ways to Cheer Yourself Up

2,002 Ways to Show Your Kids You Love Them

OTHER BOOKS BY CYNDI HAYNES
AND DALE EDWARDS

2,002 Things to Do on a Date

2,002 Ways to Say, "I Love You"

2,002 Ways to Find, Attract, and Keep a Mate

2,002 Romantic Ideas

2,002 Questions and Answers for Lovers

The Book of
FRIENDSHIP

MAKING LIFE BETTER

Cyndi Haynes

**Andrews McMeel
Publishing**

Kansas City

The Book of Friendship

01 02 03 04 05 VHG 10 9 8 7 6 5 4 3 2 1

Library of Congress Cataloging-in-Publication Data
Haynes, Cyndi.
 The book of friendship : making life better / Cyndi Haynes.
  p. cm.
 ISBN 0-7407-1156-3 (pbk.)
  1. Friendship. I. Title.

BF575.F66 H39 2001
158.2′5—dc21   00-063990

Book design by Holly Camerlinck

ATTENTION: SCHOOLS AND BUSINESSES

Andrews McMeel books are available at quantity
discounts with bulk purchase for educational, business,
or sales promotional use. For information, please write to:
Special Sales Department, Andrews McMeel Publishing,
4520 Main Street, Kansas City, Missouri 64111.

For my son and wonderful buddy, Andrew.
You have all of the qualities that I admire
most in dear friends. You are kind, wise,
loyal, and loving. I hope that your life
is always blessed with the gift
of great friendships.

ACKNOWLEDGMENTS

I wish to thank the wonderful people at
Andrews McMeel Publishing, especially my
editor, Jean Zevnik, for believing in this
book. Your hard work and support on my
behalf mean the world to me!

Dear Reader,

I can't remember a time in my life when my friends weren't important. They have brightened my path and helped carry my load every step of the way. My life has been blessed many times by their presence, probably even more than I realize.

This book is a celebration of friendship. It is also a road map to help you have better relationships and make new friends in the days ahead.

I hope this book inspires you to call old friends, appreciate your current ones, and greet with great expectation any friendships that the future holds for you.

It is also my most sincere wish that you count me as one of your friends, for if you too are deeply interested in the gift of friendship then we must be kindred spirits who just haven't met yet. I hope our paths cross soon and that our friendship will blossom.

Most warmly,

Cyndi Haynes

Qualities to Cultivate
in Yourself to
Help You Become
a Wonderful Friend

- Sense of humor
- Empathy
- Ability to keep secrets
- Sympathy
- Good listener
- Lots of interests
- Personal warmth
- Ability to laugh at yourself
- Being comfortable in your own skin
- Sense of fun
- Sense of adventure

friendship

Caring about others,

running the risk of feeling,

and leaving an impact on

people brings happiness.

—RABBI HAROLD S. KUSHNER

Why Friendship
Is So Wonderful

- It doesn't cost a cent
- It is available to all ages
- It makes those involved feel connected
to one another
- It makes us feel good about ourselves
- It gives us comfort in hard times
- It gives us someone to share our good times
- It can begin in an instant
- It can last a lifetime
- It can change your life forever

Since there is nothing
so well worth having
as friends,
never lose a chance
to make them.

— FRANCESCO GUICCIARDINI

There is only one thing
better than making
a new friend, and that is
keeping an old one.

— ELMER G. LETTERMAN

There is no physician
like a true friend.

—AUTHOR UNKNOWN

A real friend helps us
think our best thoughts,
do our noblest deeds,
be our finest selves.

—AUTHOR UNKNOWN

In reality, we are
still children.
We want to find
a playmate for
our thoughts
and feelings.

—Dr. Wilhelm Stekhel

The Twenty Most Popular Activities Worldwide That Friends Do Together

- Eat out at a restaurant
- Attend a sports event
- Shop
- Go to a bar
- Hang out
- Talk on the phone
- Go on a picnic
- Take a walk
- Attend church
- Go to a movie or play
- Exercise
- Entertain

friendship

- Meet at a coffeehouse
- Play a game of some sort
- Do crafts
- Run errands
- Participate in hobbies
- Study
- Go to a concert
- Cook

People Who Might Introduce You to Great New Friends

- Neighbors
- Significant other
- Minister, priest, or rabbi
- Mom or Dad
- Sorority or fraternity members
- Current friends
- Coworkers
- Siblings
- Aunts and uncles
- Roommates
- Former significant others
- Club members
- Fellow classmates

To like and dislike
the same things,
that is indeed
true friendship.

—SALLUST

I have friends in overalls
whose friendships
I would not swap
for the favor of
the kings of the world.

—THOMAS A. EDISON

To associate with other like-minded people in small purposeful groups is for the great majority of men and women a source of profound psychological satisfaction.

—ALDOUS HUXLEY

The worst solitude
is to be destitute
of sincere friendship.

—FRANCIS BACON

One's friends are that part
of the human race
with which one
can be human.

—GEORGE SANTAYANA

Twenty Activities to Do with Your Friends That You Might Not Have Tried Before

- Have tea at a grand hotel
- Experience the magic of the opera
- Marvel at the beauty of a ballet
- Dine at a five-star restaurant
- Attend the opening night of a play at the theater
- Meet for breakfast on a weekday
- Window-shop after the stores have closed
- Test-drive luxury cars
- Go grocery shopping at 3 A.M.
- Celebrate Friendship Day
- Take a trip

- Visit a museum or tourist attraction
- Meander through a street fair
- Take an adult-education class
- Attend an auction
- Have a picnic at sunrise
- Attend a dog show
- Tour a historic home
- Get makeovers
- Take dance lessons

The Most Common Mistakes People Make in Their Friendships

- Being defensive
- Looking for faults or problems
- Starting arguments
- Playing games
- Not being supportive of their friends' accomplishments

Friendship Trivia

The majority of husbands report that their wife
is their best friend.

The majority of wives report that their girlfriend,
not their spouse, is their best friend.

A Friend
by Any Other Name
Is Still a Friend

- Chum
- Buddy
- Pal
- Peer
- Comrade
- Partner
- Teammate
- Cohort
- Accomplice
- *Compadre*
- Crony
- Collaborator

- Confidant
  - Ally
- Sidekick
  - Mate
- Soul mate
- Messmate

The time to
make friends
is before
you need them.

—AUTHOR UNKNOWN

Learn to be silent.
Let your quiet mind
listen and absorb.

—PYTHAGORAS

Friendship 101

Be interested—don't try to be interesting.

Be pleasing—don't expect to be pleased.

Be entertaining—don't wait to be entertained.

Be lovable—don't wait to be loved.

Be helpful—don't ask to be helped.

—AUTHOR UNKNOWN

A friend is
a lot of things,
but a critic he isn't.

—BERNX WILLIAMS

Friends are made
by many acts
and lost by only one.

—AUTHOR UNKNOWN

A man who would
have many friends
must show himself friendly.

—JEWISH SAYING

We are all connected
in the great circle of life.

—MUFASA, *THE LION KING*

The older you get,
the more you realize
that kindness
is synonymous
with happiness.

—LIONEL BARRYMORE

Instinct teaches us
to look for happiness
outside ourselves.

—BLAISE PASCAL

How to Build Fabulous Rapport with Others

• Match their body language

• Listen to the tone of the other person's voice
and try to match it closely

• Ask for their help

• Find a common ground

• Listen more and talk less

• Ask questions

• Enjoy being in someone else's company and let it show

• Express your friendship in the ways that
matter to your friends

The Most Common Things That People Look for in Opposite-Sex Friends

- Advice on their love lives
- A different perspective on life
- Career advice
- The brother or sister they never had
- Fashion advice
- Shared interests
- Partner for sports
- Dance partner
- Fun
- Companionship
- Nurturing
- Future romantic partner

- Networking connection
- Future business partner
- Shopping partner

The best mirror is an old friend.

—AUTHOR UNKNOWN

No one person can possibly
combine all the elements
supposed to make up
what everyone means
by friendship.

— FRANCIS MARION
CRAWFORD

Friendship is like money,
easier made than kept.

— AUTHOR UNKNOWN

A man is known
by the company
he keeps.

— AUTHOR UNKNOWN

Accident counts
for much
in companionship
as in marriage.

—HENRY ADAMS

You cannot be friends
upon any other terms
than upon the terms
of equality.

—WOODROW WILSON

The proper office of a friend
is to side with you when
you are in the wrong.
Nearly everybody will
side with you when you
are in the right.

—MARK TWAIN

Live so that your
friends can defend you,
but never have to.

—ARNOLD GLASGOW

Five years from now you will
be pretty much the same as you
are today except for two things:
the books you read and the
people you get close to.

—CHARLES JONES

friendship

Basic Advice for Office Friendships

- Be discreet
- Examine your motives for wanting to be friends with a particular person
- Ask yourself what would happen if the friendship ended
- Be careful of office gossip
- Never confide *anything* that would hurt your career

But every road is tough to me,
That has no one to cheer it.

—ELIZABETH SHANE

Tell me thy
company, and I'll
tell thee
what thou art.

—Miguel de Cervantes

A sympathetic friend
can be quite as dear
as a brother.

—Homer

Prosperity makes friends,
adversity tries them.

—PUBLILIUS SYRUS

Be slow to fall into
friendship; but when
thou are in, continue firm
and constant.

—SOCRATES

In prosperity
our friends know us;
in adversity we know
our friends.

—JOHN CHURTON COLLINS

The man who trusts
other men will make
fewer mistakes than he
who distrusts them.

—CAMILLO DI CAVOUR

The language
of friendship
is not words,
but meanings.

—HENRY DAVID THOREAU

Friendship needs
no words—it is
solitude delivered from
the anguish of loneliness.

—DAG HAMMARSKJÖLD

Surround Yourself with Friends That

- Build you up
- Listen
- Give back
- Tell the whole truth
- Empathize with you
- Understand you
- Support you
- Respect you
- Truly care about your welfare

Ways to Have Great Long-Distance Friendships

• Contact each other often by phone

• Send cards

• Send small gifts that carry a special meaning to your pal

• Arrange frequent get-togethers

• Send photos

• E-mail regularly

• Take trips together

friendship

I believe that we are always
attracted to what we need most,
an instinct leading us towards
the persons who are to open
new vistas in our lives and fill
them with new knowledge.

—HELENE ISWOLSKI

The growth
of true friendship
may be a
lifelong affair.

—SARAH ORNE JEWETT

He who hath
many friends,
hath none.

—ARISTOTLE

Old friends are best.
King James used to call for
his old shoes; they were easiest
to his feet.

—JOHN SELDEN

The Most Talked About Subjects Among Female Friends

- Relationships
- Children
- Female health issues
- Work
- Other friends' lives
- Fashion trends

friendship

The Most Talked About Subjects Among Male Friends

- Sports
- Politics
- Investments
- Cars
- Work
- Women

Life is partly
what we make it,
and partly what it
is made by
the friends
we choose.

—TEHYI HSIEH

Friendships aren't perfect and yet they are very precious. For me, not expecting perfection all in one place was a great release.

—LETTY COTTIN POGREBIN

Loyalty is what we seek
in friendship.

—CICERO

To throw away
an honest friend is,
as it were,
to throw your life away.

—SOPHOCLES

Thine own friend,
and thy father's friend,
forsake not.

—Proverbs 27:10

If you want
an accounting
of your worth,
count your friends.

—Merry Browne

To have a good friend is one
of the highest delights of life;
to be a good friend is one of
the noblest and most difficult
undertakings.

—AUTHOR UNKNOWN

Important Ways
to Improve
Your Friendships

- Stop trying to change your friends
- Appreciate all of the good things that your friends bring to your life
- Approach any trouble spots diplomatically
- Arrange to do something meaningful together
- Spend more/less time together
- Forgive past transgressions—start anew
- Break out of your routines
- Communicate from the heart

Your closest
relationships
seem to matter most
for your health.

—DR. JANICE KIECOLT-GLASER

The Things That Children Want Most in Their Friendships

- Someone to play with
- Someone to talk to
- Someone to go places with
- Someone to have fun with
- Someone to share their lives with

Adults want the same things!

The Trickiest Topics
for Friends to Discuss

- Personal finances
- Personal grooming habits
- Details of one's love life
- Skeletons in one's closest
- The cost of one's belongings

The Most Common Differences Between School Chums and After-College Pals

- Not as much time spent together as people grow older
- Friendships may not be as intense
- Friends not as accessible
- Friendships are harder to maintain
- New friendships are more difficult to make since you aren't always with similar people as you were in your school days

The Twenty Characteristics That Women Want Most in Their Closest Friends

- Friendliness
- Trustworthiness
- Generosity
- Intelligence
- Caring
- Enthusiasm
- Morality
- Fashionableness
- Cheerfulness
- Sensitivity
- Graciousness

- Helpfulness

- Truthfulness

- Fun to be around

- Good self-esteem

- Intuitiveness

- Patience

- Poise

- Loyalty

- Kindness

The Twenty Characteristics That Men Want Most in Their Closest Friends

- Focus
- Humility
- Frankness
- Good-naturedness
- Practicality
- Likability
- Groundedness
- Industriousness
- Imaginativeness
- Open-mindedness
- Honesty

- Bravery
- Generosity
- Easygoingness
- Ethicality
- Diplomacy
- Coolness/debonairness
- Directness
- Humor
- Discreetness

Acquaintance I would have,
but when it depends
not on the number,
but the choice of friends.

—ABRAHAM COWLEY

How often we find ourselves
turning our backs on
our actual friends, that we
may go and meet their
ideal cousins.

—HENRY DAVID THOREAU

As there are some flowers which you should smell but slightly to extract all that is pleasant in them . . . so there are some men with whom a slight acquaintance is quite sufficient to draw out all that is agreeable; a more intimate one would be unsafe and unsatisfactory.

—WALTER SAVAGE LANDOR

Sudden friendship,
sure repentance.

—AUTHOR UNKNOWN

A man becomes
like those
whose society
he loves.

—HINDU PROVERB

If you always live with those
who are lame, you will yourself
learn to limp.

—Latin proverb

Wonderful Ways to Help a Friend Celebrate Good News

- Be genuinely happy for her
- Write a letter to him
- Send a meaningful gift
- Send a thoughtful card
- Take her out to dinner to celebrate
- Throw a party for him
- Give her a gigantic hug
- Give him a meaningful book
- Arrange a special celebration dinner for her
  and her significant other
- Send a bottle of champagne

friendship

• Call her mom and plan a family celebration party for her

• Take him to lunch and invite all of his friends

• Take her to dinner and invite her coworkers

• Send her a fabulous bouquet of her favorite flowers

Activities to Do with Your Friends That Can Make Our World a Little Bit Better

- Donate blood together
- Rescue a dog from the pound
- Tutor underprivileged kids
- Team up to do volunteer work
- Run in a charity race
- Pick up litter
- Assist with the Special Olympics
- Work at a soup kitchen
- Visit a nursing home on your lunch hours

- Support the Heifer Project through your financial contributions
- Become Big Sisters or Big Brothers together
- Recycle your newspapers and cans
- Help each other clean out closets and donate the old items to charity

Silences make the
real conversations between
friends. Not the saying
but the never needing to say
is what counts.

—AUTHOR UNKNOWN

Friendship consists
in forgetting what one gives
and remembering
what one receives.

—DUMAS THE YOUNGER

Go often to the house of thy friend
for weeds choke up the unused path.

— AUTHOR UNKNOWN

Friendship is the
only cement
that will ever hold
the world together.

—Author unknown

How to Quickly
Beat Loneliness

• Reach deep inside to find your own inner strength

• Know that you are good company and that
you have a lot to offer to others

• Stop obsessing over your feeling of loneliness

• Fill your mind with uplifting, fun, and creative thoughts

• Reach out to others, especially those in need

• Search out other lonely people

• Try to make others happy

• Do different things, vary your routines

• Stop being a couch potato

• Create a plan for relieving your loneliness

• Remember that you are never truly alone,
for God is always with you

Thoughts for Success

When you meet a new group of people, focus on the one
person that you would like to get to know the most

When you are first introduced to someone, repeat that person's
name to help you remember it

Get the correct pronunciation of a person's name when you
first meet

Ask people about their lives, loves, and dreams

To keep yourself from being boring, stay up on current
affairs and pop culture

friendship

Always make sure that you have the correct spelling of your friend's name when you mail something to her

Write thank-you notes for all gifts and special favors

Do favors for your friends

Write letters of appreciation

Remember your friends' holidays that are different from your own

Count your friends among the greatest blessings in your life

The Top Twenty Places Where People Make New Friends

- Work
- Church
- Fitness centers
- Professional organizations
- Social clubs
- Mothers' support groups
- On-line
- Hobby-related activities
- Volunteering
- In their neighborhoods
- Sports events or playing sports

friendship

- Travel

- Hair salons

- Adult-education classes and events

- Coffeehouses

- Trade shows

- Golf lessons

- Tennis lessons

- Spas

- Parties

If a man does not make
new acquaintances as he
advances through life, he will
soon find himself alone.

—SAMUEL JOHNSON

A friendship founded
on business
is a good deal better
than a business
founded on friendship.

—JOHN D. ROCKEFELLER

Do good to thy friend
to keep him—
to thine enemy to gain him.

— BEN FRANKLIN

The depth of a friendship—
how much it means to us . . .
depends, at least in part, upon
how many parts of ourselves
a friend sees, shares,
and validates.

— LILLIAN RUBIN

Friendship improves
happiness, and
abates misery,
by doubling our joy,
and dividing
our grief.

—JOSEPH ADDISON

Reprove a friend
in secret,
but praise him
before others.

—Author unknown

Treat your friend
as if he might
become an enemy.

—Publilius Syrus

We can make more enemies
by what we say
than friends
by what we do.

—JOHN CHURTON COLLINS

A friend is a person
with whom you can dare
to be yourself.

—AUTHOR UNKNOWN

Thy friend has
a friend, and
thy friend's friend
has a friend.
Be discreet.

—THE TALMUD

Let us be the first to give
a friendly sign, to nod first,
smile first, speak first,
and—if such a thing
is necessary—forgive first.

—AUTHOR UNKNOWN

We know what
a person thinks not when
he tells us what he thinks,
but by his actions.

—ISAAC BASHEVIS SINGER

Friend:
one who knows
all about you
and likes you
just the same.

—ELBERT HUBBARD

Phrases to Use Often with Your Friends

- I'm glad to see you
- You did a great job
- I believe in you
- If you need help, just ask
- How can I be of service to you?
- I appreciate what you did for me
- Thanks
- Please
- I love you
- I am proud to be your friend
- I'm sorry

friendship

Friendship Trivia

You have over six billion people on this planet to choose from when picking out a new friend.

How to Be Good Friends with Your Roommate

• Respect each other's privacy

• Promptly give each other phone messages, mail, etc.

• Meet all of your financial responsibilities

• Be tidy

• Be cheerful

• Learn the fine art of sharing

• Look past each other's faults

• Be nice to each other's friends and relatives

• Knock

• Keep abreast of each other's schedules

• Go out together for fun times

• Talk openly about your differences

• Make sure that she knows that you want to be friends

friendship

Connections
are made slowly,
sometimes they
grow underground.

—MARGE PIERCY

Areas That Need to Be Discussed Before Friends Become Roommates

- Finances
- Domestic chores
- Schedules
- Expectations
- Friends and relatives
- Leisure-time activities
- Entertaining
- Privacy issues
- Decorating

friendship

In judging others,
folks will work overtime
for no pay.

—Charles Edwin Carrithers

Let everyone
be swift to hear;
slow to speak;
slow to wrath.

—James 1:19

Ten Great Ways to Help a Friend in Trouble

- Keep calling and checking on her
- Treat her to a little extra pampering
- Overlook her moodiness
- Encourage her to have a social life
- Set up regular get-togethers with her
- Take care of her children and pets
- Help with her household chores
- Send a meaningful card or gift
- Send a "Cry Till You Dry" gift box and fill it with a lace hankie, journal, beautiful pen, and chocolates
- Help her find the right professional to help solve her crisis if one is needed, such as a therapist, lawyer, or banker

friendship

To lose a friend
is the greatest
of all losses.

—Publilius Syrus

How casually and
unobservedly we make
all our most valued
acquaintances.

—Ralph Waldo Emerson

What hat causes us to like new acquaintances is not so much weariness of our old ones, or the pleasure of change, as disgust at not being sufficiently admired by those who know us too well, and the hope of being admired more by those who do not know so much about us.

—FRANÇOIS
DE LA ROCHEFOUCAULD

Rather throw away
that which is
dearest to you,
your own life,
than turn away
a good friend.

—SOPHOCLES

Activities to Do with Your Friend That Can Improve *Your* World

• Attend church

• Take adult-education classes

• Redecorate your home or office

• Learn a new skill

• Relax

• Join a health club

• Go on a diet

• Give up smoking

• Get a makeover

• Start a book club

• Become roomies

- Play matchmaker for each other
- Share secrets that are troubling to you
- Help plan each other's future
- Set goals and help each other reach them
- Dream big
- Spend more time outdoors
- Put more fun in your life

Many a friendship—long,
loyal, and self-sacrificing—
rested at first upon no
thicker a foundation than
a kind word.

—FREDERICK W. FABER

No act of kindness
is wasted.

—WILLIAM PURKEY

The only reward of virtue
is virtue; the only way to
have a friend is to be
a true friend.

—RALPH WALDO EMERSON

Trouble is a great sieve
through which we sift
our acquaintances;
those who are too big
to pass through are friends.

—NORTH CAROLINA CHURCHMAN

A real friend is one who will
tell you of your faults and
follies in prosperity, and assist
you with his hand and heart in
adversity.

—AUTHOR UNKNOWN

The Twenty Trickiest Friendship Situations

- A friend gives you a gift and you don't have one for her
- Your friend is very moody
- A friend wants to borrow money and you don't want to lend it
- Your friend is jealous of your success
- Your friend flirts with your sweetie
- Your friend has become a stay-at-home mom and you are an avid career woman without kids
- Your friend wants too much of your time
- Your friend critiques you too much
- You don't like your friend's significant other
- Your pal has become a slob
- Your friend's sweetie is cheating on her and you know it, but she doesn't

- Your other friends don't like her
- Your friend doesn't like your other friends
- Your friend is gravely ill and it scares you
- Your friend is getting a divorce and you want to stay friends with her ex
- Your friend exaggerates tremendously
- Your friend snubs you when she is with another pal
- Your friend has a drug or alcohol problem
- Your friend breaks a confidence
- You want to end the friendship

Quick Way to Solve Friendship Troubles

- Define the problem

- Brainstorm solutions

- Refrain from hasty responses

- Weigh all options

- Communicate from the heart and head

Great souls by instinct to each other turn,
Demand alliance, and in friendship burn.

—JOSEPH ADDISON

Friendship is composed of a single soul inhabiting two bodies.

—ARISTOTLE

Gently to hear,
kindly to judge.

—WILLIAM SHAKESPEARE

Sharing a bit
of friendliness with others
does not impoverish
a man.

—AUTHOR UNKNOWN

So long as we love, we serve.
So long as we are loved by
others we are indispensable;
and no man is useless while
he has a friend.

—ROBERT LOUIS STEVENSON

True friendship is like
sound health, the value
of it is seldom known
until it is lost.

— C. C. COLTON

Do not judge
your friend
until you stand
in his place.

— AUTHOR UNKNOWN

Charm:
The ability to make someone else think that both of you are pretty wonderful.

—AUTHOR UNKNOWN

Want to Know What Being Friendly Feels Like? Try Being

- Conciliatory
- Genial
- Agreeable
- Helpful
- Kind
- Cordial
- Amicable
- Affable
- Sympathetic
- Social
- Attentive
- Solicitous

friendship

The best way
to keep your friends
is not to give them away.

—WILSON MIZNER

Hold a true friend
with both your hands.

—NIGERIAN PROVERB

We often choose a friend

as we do a mistress, for no

particular excellence in

themselves, but merely from

some circumstance that flatters

our self-love.

—WILLIAM HAZLITT

To be capable of steady friendship or lasting love are the two greatest proofs, not only of goodness of heart, but of strength of mind.

—WILLIAM HAZLITT

One enemy
is too many;
a hundred friends
too few.

—AUTHOR UNKNOWN

Wonderful Ideas
for Small or
Unexpected Gifts

- Homemade goodies
- Coupon book of favors to do for your friend
- Magazine subscriptions
- Self-help books or tapes
- CDs
- Spa gift certificates
- Salon gift certificates
- Tickets to an upcoming event
- Music boxes with a special song
- Teddy bear
- Homemade gift
- Wonderful novel or mystery
- Gifts from your travels

- Gifts for your friend's child or pet

- Stationery

- Lotions, bath gels, or beauty treatments

- Trendy gadgets

- Books about friendship

- Ties, hats, gloves in a distinctive style

- Framed photo of you and your friend

I never enter a new company without the hope that I may discover a friend, perhaps the friend, sitting there with an expectant smile. That hope survives a thousand disappointments.

—ARTHUR CHRISTOPHER
BENSON

The Most Popular Reasons Why Adults Say That Moms Make Great Pals

- Nobody knows them better
- Mom knows their entire life story
- She loves them no matter what happens
- She wants the best for them
- They have lots of things in common

The Most Popular Reasons Why Adults Say That Dads Make Great Pals

• He loves them

• He has a vested interest in their success

• He has been a role model for them

• He shares their history

• He makes them feel safe

To find a friend
one must close one eye—
to keep a friend, two.

—AUTHOR UNKNOWN

No man is a failure
who has friends.

—CLARENCE, GEORGE BAILEY'S ANGEL IN
IT'S A WONDERFUL LIFE

Being able to feel the pain
of others is a strength.
It gives us incentive
to avoid causing pain.

—MORGAN LLYWELYN

A true friend
is the best possession.

—AUTHOR UNKNOWN

When a friend is in trouble,

don't annoy him by asking if

there is anything you can do.

Think up something

appropriate and do it.

—EDGAR WATSON HOWE

He does good
to himself
who does good
to his friend.

—ERASMUS

A friend
is like a poem.

—PERSIAN PROVERB

None is so rich
as to throw away
a friend.

—TURKISH PROVERB

To be social
is to be forgiving.

—ROBERT FROST

Great Seasonal Activities for Friends to Do Together

Springtime

- Plant flowers

- Stroll outdoors

- Play tennis or golf

- Shop for new clothes

- Double-date—everyone falls in love in the spring

Summer

- Go boating

- Take a vacation

- Help each other adopt a homeless pet

- Watch a ball game

- Entertain

Fall

- Go to a football game

- Take a fall-foliage drive

- Shop for new clothes

- Attend a class

- Plan a great reunion with old pals

Wintertime

- Go Christmas shopping

- Decorate together for the holidays

- Throw a fabulous party

- Enjoy a sleigh ride

- Participate in a winter sport

A true friend is the greatest of all blessings, and that which we take the least care of all to acquire.

—FRANÇOIS
DE LA ROCHEFOUCAULD

There is magic in the memory of a schoolboy friendship. It softens the heart, and even affects the nervous system of those who have no heart.

—Benjamin Disraeli

Without wearing any mask
we are conscious of,
we have a special face
for each friend.

—OLIVER WENDELL HOLMES

Ah, how good it feels!
The hand
of an old friend.

—HENRY WADSWORTH LONGFELLOW

The most called upon
prerequisite of a friend
is an accessible ear.

—MAYA ANGELOU

The balm of life,
a kind
and faithful friend.

—MERCY OTIS WARREN

It is not how we look that is important. What really counts is to be as sunny as possible inside; then no one stops long to look at the outside.

—JOHNNY GRUELLE

It is one of
    the blessings of
old friends that you
    can afford to be
stupid with them.

—RALPH WALDO EMERSON

Famous Friends

- Oprah Winfrey and Gayle King
- Charlie Brown and the whole Peanuts gang
- Winnie-the-Pooh and Christopher Robin
- Chip and Dale
- Rosie O'Donnell and Madonna
- Mickey Mouse and Minnie Mouse
- Tom and Jerry
- Bullwinkle and Rocky
- Underdog and Sweet Polly Purebread
- Clark Kent and Lois Lane
- Lucy and Ethel, *I Love Lucy* television show
- Nancy Drew, Bess, and George
- Ben & Jerry
- Simon & Garfunkel

Ten More Ways to Help a Friend in Trouble

- Invite her to stay with you
- Cry with her
- Give her a good reason to smile and laugh
- Call her sister, mother, or other friends to help her
- Exercise with her
- Celebrate all of the good things left in her life
- Find a support group for her
- Find any on-line resources that would help her
- Hug her often
- Give her appropriate self-help books

friendship

The art of friendship
has been little cultivated
in our society.

—Robert J. Havighurst

When you meet anyone,
just stop and think, "How
can I show this person that
I am a friend?" A little teeny
voice inside you will tell you
just how you can do it.

—Johnny Gruelle

Human beings are born into
this little span of life of which
the best thing is its friendships
and intimacies . . . and yet they
leave their friendships and
intimacies with no cultivation,
to grow as they will by the
roadside, expecting them to
"keep" by force of mere inertia.

—WILLIAM JAMES

It is better
in times of need
to have a friend
rather than money.

—GREEK PROVERB

Friendship Trivia

More friendships end during a friend's period
of good fortune than during times of
great turmoil.

The friend of my adversity I shall always cherish most. I can better trust those who have helped to relieve the gloom of my dark hours than those who are so ready to enjoy with me the sunshine of my prosperity.

—ULYSSES S. GRANT

I loathe a friend . . . who takes his friend's prosperity but will not voyage with him in his grief.

—EURIPIDES

One loyal friend
is worth
ten thousand relatives.

—EURIPIDES

He alone
has lost the art to live
who cannot win
new friends.

—SILAS WEIR MITCHELL

One who's our friend is fond
of us; one who's fond of us isn't
necessarily our friend.

—LUCIUS ANNAEUS SENECA

Have no friends
not equal to yourself.

—Confucius

Be a friend to thyself,
and others will be so, too.

—Thomas Fuller

The Easiest Ways
for the Career-Minded
to Make New Friends

- Network
- Join professional organizations
- Become friends with your coworkers
- Entertain regularly
- Attend lectures and seminars of interest

You meet your friend,
your face brightens—
you have struck gold.

—KASSIA

Great friendship
is never
without anxiety.

—MARQUISE DE SÉVIGNÉ

The company
makes the feast.

—AUTHOR UNKNOWN

The holy passion of
friendship is of so sweet and
steady and loyal and enduring a
nature that it will last through a
whole lifetime, if not asked to
lend money.

—MARK TWAIN

With money you can
buy all of the friends
you want, but they are
never worth the price.

—AUTHOR UNKNOWN

Friendship is love
without wings.

—LORD BYRON

Shared joys make a friend,
not shared sufferings.

—FRIEDRICH NIETZSCHE

When our friends are alive,
we see the good qualities
they lack; dead, we
remember only those
they possessed.

—J. PETET-SENN

Friendship is only
a reciprocal conciliation
of interests.

—FRANÇOIS DE LA ROCHEFOUCAULD

A homemade friend
wears longer
than one you buy
in the market.

—AUSTIN O'MALLEY

Friendship Trivia

According to recent studies,
the average woman's friendship lasts
a little over three years and the average
man's friendship lasts over five years.

The Most Important Qualities Found in Friendships That Have Lasted a Decade or Longer

- Sense of humor
- The ability to look past another's shortcomings
- Making the effort to get together regularly
- Always being supportive in good times and bad times
- Sharing many parts of each other's lives
- Communicating effectively

Affirmations for Becoming a Good-Quality Friend

- I treat all of my friends with respect and kindness

- I practice the Golden Rule

- I am always loyal

- I am empathetic and understanding

- I am a good listener

- I am trustworthy and my friends can always count on me

- I realize that all friends are gifts from God and I treasure their presence in my world

- People are more important to me than things

- I take the time to be a good friend to all of my chums

- I never take any of my friends for granted

We have two ears
and one mouth
so that we can listen
twice as much
as we speak.

—EPICTETUS

Ways to Feel Better After a Fight with a Friend

- Take a long hot shower
- Call another friend
- Exercise
- Call your mom
- Call a sibling
- Take your dog for a walk
- Cry and get out the hurt
- Write down your feelings in a journal
- Write a letter to your friend
- Get a massage

- Write a love letter to yourself stating why you are still a good person to have as a friend

- Call your friend

- Pray

- Forgive and forget

friendship

Friends are
a second existence.

—Baltasar Gracián y Morales

Four be the things
I am wiser to know:
Idleness, sorrow, a friend,
and a foe.

—Author unknown

Make all good men your
well-wishers, and then, in the
years' steady sifting, some of
them will turn into friends.

—JOHN HAY

Friendship is seldom lasting
but between equals, or where
the superiority on one side is
reduced by some equivalent
advantage on the other.

—SAMUEL JOHNSON

A friend should be
a master at guessing
and keeping still.

—FRIEDRICH NIETZSCHE

A man's growth
is seen in the
successive choirs
of his friends.

—RALPH WALDO EMERSON

Prosperity is not
a just scale;
adversity is the only balance
to weigh friends.

—PLUTARCH

'Tis the privilege
of friendship
to talk nonsense,
and have her
nonsense respected.

—CHARLES LAMB

Friendship is
the pleasing game
of interchanging
praise.

—OLIVER WENDELL HOLMES

The Qualities That People Want Most in Their Lifetime Friend (Otherwise Known as Their Marriage Partner)

- Lovingness
- Supportiveness
- Intelligence
- Integrity
- Sense of humor
- Good sense of fun
- Loyalty
- Politeness
- Happiness
- Openness

- Generosity
- Affectionateness
- Understanding
- Empathy
- Patience
- Lightheartedness

friendship

And we find at the end of a perfect day,
The soul of a friend we've made.

—CARRIE JACOBS BOND

A man should keep his friendships in constant repair.

—Samuel Johnson

You have your money and your friend,

You loan your money to your friend,

You ask your money from your friend,

You lose your money and your friend.

— AUTHOR UNKNOWN

Never explain—
your friends
do not need it,
and your enemies
will not believe it.

—AUTHOR UNKNOWN

How to Become
Friends with God

- Pray a lot

- Trust

- Read spiritual books

- Seek Him

- Look for miracles happening all around you

- Affirm that He is with you

- View prayer as two-way communication

- Listen to spiritual music

- Make a religious pilgrimage

- Count your blessings

- Attend religious services regularly

- Talk to God as you would a friend

- Celebrate religious holidays

- Associate with spiritual people
  - Seek His guidance and help
  - Open up your heart to Him

Spend an Evening Every Month Doing Friendship-Building Activities Like:

• Locating old friends on the Internet

• Joining a club to meet new friends

• Writing to current pals

• Faxing kind words to friends

• Sending cartoons or articles of importance to your pals

• Calling friends just to say "Hello"

• Making social plans

The better part
of one's life
consists of his friendships.

—ABRAHAM LINCOLN

The richer your friends,
the more they will cost you.

—ELIZABETH MARBURY

How to Be Friends with Your Ex, *If* You Want to Be

- Forgive and forget
- Set emotional boundaries
- Respect each other's privacy
- Keep things light and simple
- Give up all romantic expectations

No man can be happy
without a friend, nor be
sure of his friend till
he is unhappy.

—THOMAS FULLER

Old friends are the
great blessing of one's
later years. . . . They have
a memory of the
same events and have
the same mode of thinking.

—HORACE WALPOLE

How to Be Friends with Your Parents

- Look at them as people, not just as your parents
- Treat them with the same respect that you show all your other friends
- Plan fun outings
- Listen to their point of view
- Communicate openly and honestly
- Work at this relationship
- Include them in many different areas of your life

The Easiest Ways for Older People to Make New Friends

- Join a new club

- Do volunteer work

- Take a class

- Entertain and have old friends bring their friends

- Travel with large groups of people

Little Acts of Kindness That Go a Long Way in the Friendship Lane

- Pick up the check at dinner when
  you eat out with your friend

- Send thank-you notes for all gifts and acts
  of special consideration

- Run errands for your pals

- Baby-sit for your friend's children

- Pet-sit for your friend's furry buddy

- Go along on a scary doctor or dentist appointment and
  give your pal emotional support

- Pick up your chum at the airport

- Help your friend throw a great party

- Place pictures of your friends around your home

- Attend your friends' children's games and recitals
  - House-sit for a vacationing buddy
  - Set her up with Mr. Right
  - Tell her when she is dating Mr. Wrong

Animals are such agreeable friends—they ask no questions, they pass no criticisms.

— GEORGE ELIOT

Wonderful Gift Ideas
for a Very
Special Friend

• Bottle of fine wine from the year of his birth

• Gift certificate for a getaway weekend

• Antique jewelry with an extraordinary past

• Gold friendship bracelet

• Sterling picture frame with a photo of the two of you

• First edition of a favorite book

• Watercolor of your friend's home or pet

• Generous donation in your friend's honor to
the charity of her choice

• Fine leather briefcase

- Any extravagance that you know that your friend would love
- Tickets to a favorite event
- Dinner for two at a five-star restaurant
- New puppy from an animal shelter if she has been longing for a pet

There is space within sisterhood for likeness and difference, for the subtle differences that challenge and delight; there is space for disappointment—and surprise.

— CHRISTINE DOWNING

In times of great anxiety we can draw power from our friends. We should at times, however, avoid friends who sympathize too deeply, who give us pity rather than strength.

—D. PUPTON

I am treating you as my friend,
asking you to share my present
minuses in the hope I can ask
you to share my future pluses.

—KATHERINE MANSFIELD

Any man will usually get
from other men what he is
expecting from them. If he is
looking for friendship, he will
likely receive it. If his attitude is
that of indifference, it will beget
indifference. And if a man is
looking for a fight, he will in all
likelihood be accommodated in
that.

—JOHN RICHELSEN

Friends are
the sunshine of life.

—JOHN HAY

Of course you
can go home again!
You just look in your heart
for your old best friend.

—HELEN MOSS

Holiday Activities to Share with Friends

Chinese New Year

- Parades
- Festive dinner

Birthdays

- Parties
- Cards/gifts
- Lunches
- Dinners

New Year's Eve and New Year's Day

- Parties
- Resolution making

Super Bowl Sunday

- Parties

- Watching or attending the game and all the surrounding events
- Giving up and going shopping

Valentine's Day

- No date? Celebrate together
- Double date
- Shop together for your significant others' gifts

Presidents' Day

- Shop the sales together

Passover

- Attend a Passover celebration at a synagogue or temple together
- Attend a seder together

Easter

- Attend religious services
- Make baskets for your children

- Shop for your spring wardrobe together
- Cook a holiday feast together

Mother's Day

- Take your moms to lunch together
- Send her a card if she is a mom

Memorial Day

- Picnic together
- Go on a getaway together
- Plan fun outdoor activities

Father's Day

- Take your dads out for dinner together
- Send him a card if he is a dad

Fourth of July

- Attend a big fireworks display
- Entertain
- Vacation together

Labor Day

- Enjoy the last weekend of summertime together
- Shop for fall clothes together
- Take a long weekend trip together

Halloween

- Throw a great costume party together
- Decorate for fall together
- Make costumes for your children together
- Act like kids together

Thanksgiving

- Cook dinner together
- Appreciate each other's friendship
- Count your blessings with each other

Hanukkah

- Attend a Hanukkah celebration at a synagogue
  or temple together

- Shop for gifts for your family together
- Exchange gifts

Christmas

- Shop for gifts for each other
- Shop together
- Wrap presents together
- Attend parties together
- Entertain together
- Bake cookies together
- Window-shop together
- Drive around to see all of the lights and holiday displays together
- Worship together
- Remember the true meaning of Christmas together

Kwanza

- Attend family and friends' gatherings

The Easiest Ways
to Be Friends with
Your Siblings

- Forgive and forget the past

- Stop comparing yourselves

- Treat each other like friends

- Act as equals even if you weren't treated
  that way growing up

- Relax and let the friendship evolve in its own way

- Communicate openly and from the heart

- Solve any disputes without parental intervention
  having to take place

friendship

The most important single
influence in the life of a person
is another person . . . who is
worthy of emulation.

—PAUL D. SHAFER

How to Be a
Great Friend to
Your Animal Buddies

- Always treat them kindly

- Remember to serve their meals on time

- Take them on safe, fun outings

- Provide water, shelter, and health care

- Exercise together

- Play together every day

- Snuggle daily

- Give birthday gifts and Christmas gifts

- Watch their weight

friendship

Confidence is
the foundation
of friendship.
If we give it,
we will receive it.

—HARRY E. HUMPHREY, JR.

It is good enough
that I am of value
to somebody today.

—HUGH PRATHER

One who knows how
to show and to accept
kindness will be a friend
better than any possession.

— SOPHOCLES

Some of my best friends
are illusions.
Been sustaining them
for years.

— SHEILA BALLANTYNE

If you will listen
you will double
your charisma.

—DAVID NIVEN

To accept a favor
from a friend
is to confer one.

—JOHN CHURTON COLLINS

Friendship with oneself
is all-important, because
without it one cannot
be friends with anyone else.

—ELEANOR ROOSEVELT

True friends . . . face in
the same direction,
toward common projects,
interests, goals.

—C. S. LEWIS

It is not so much
our friends' help
that helps us,
as the confidence
of their help.

—EPICURUS

When one friend
washes another,
both become clean.

—DUTCH PROVERB

We challenge one another
to be funnier and smarter . . .
It's the way friends make
love to one another.

—ANNIE GOTTLIEB

Affinities are rare.
They come but a few times
in a life. It is awful to risk
losing one when it arrives.

—FLORENCE H. WINTERBURN

Associate yourself
with men of good quality
if you esteem your own
reputation, for 'tis
better to be alone
than in bad company.

—GEORGE WASHINGTON

A hedge between
keeps friendships green.

—AUTHOR UNKNOWN

Ways to Make Friends with People of Different Ages, Backgrounds, Interests, Etc.

- Reach out to people in need
- Join groups whose members are not in your normal social range
- Attend church functions
- Become friends with your coworkers' friends and family
- Make friends with your family's friends
- Do volunteer work
- Reach out to your neighbors
- Take up a new sport or hobby

Men only become friends by community of pleasures.

—Samuel Johnson

I have always differentiated between two types of friends: those who want proofs of friendship, and those who do not. One kind loves me for myself, and the others for themselves.

—GÉRARD DE NERVAL

friendship

There is a definite process by which one made people into friends, and it involved talking to them and listening to them for hours at a time.

—REBECCA WEST

Of all of the things which
wisdom provides to make life
entirely happy, much the
greatest is the possession of
friendship.

—EPICURUS

How to Overcome Shyness—the Great Stumbling Block to Friendship

- Relax
- Take the focus off yourself by thinking about the other person
- Breathe deeply
- Detach—look at social situations realistically
- Make the first move in a friendship
- Smile
- Remember to be yourself; no one else can do it just the way you can
- Exercise regularly to get rid of stress in your body
- Wear clothes that make you feel good about yourself

- Role-play with other shy friends for upcoming social events
- If shyness is crippling you socially, seek help from a qualified professional

True friendship
is self-love
at second hand.

—WILLIAM HAZLITT

If a man is
worth knowing at all,
he is worth knowing well.

—ALEXANDER SMITH

Many a person has held
close, throughout their entire
lives, two friends that always
remained strange to one
another, because one of them
attracted by virtue of similarity,
the other by difference.

—EMIL LUDWIG

How to Keep Your Friendships Growing and Getting Better Year After Year

- Go to new places

- Talk about new subjects

- Try different activities

- Vary the time of day that you get together

- Invite exciting people to join you

- Read current best-sellers and discuss them

- Travel together

- Entertain together

- Vary the day of the week that you see each other

- Double-date

Keep away from people who try to belittle your ambitions. Small people always do that, but the really great make you feel that you, too, can become great.

—MARK TWAIN

friendship

The Most Common Things That Friends Fight About

- An unkind remark
- Favors not repaid
- Things borrowed and not returned or returned in poor condition
- Not being included at a special event
- Breaking a confidence
- Trying to move in on a friend's love interest
- Being the topic of your friend's gossip
- The friend not helping during a difficult time
- Moodiness
- Money
- Being late

Qualities That Ruin Friendships

- Disloyalty

- Rudeness

- Arrogance

- Being cheap

- Prying

- Self-centeredness

- Always being late

Friendship is a union
of spirits, a marriage
of hearts, and the
bond there of virtue.

—SAMUEL JOHNSON

I like a highland friend
who will stand by me
not only when I am
in the right, but when I am
a little in the wrong.

—SIR WALTER SCOTT

It is characteristic of spontaneous friendship to take on, without inquiry and almost at first sight, the unseen doings and unspoken sentiments of our friends; the part known gives us evidence enough that the unknown part cannot be much amiss.

—GEORGE SANTAYANA

Books and friends should be few but good.

—AUTHOR UNKNOWN

Friendship is a plant which must be often watered.

—AUTHOR UNKNOWN

The first thing to learn in intercourse with others is non-interference with their own peculiar ways of being happy, provided those ways do not assume to interfere with ours.

—WILLIAM JAMES

That friendship may be at once fond and lasting, there must not only be equal virtue on each part, but virtue of the same kind; not only the same end must be proposed, but the same means must be approved by both.

—SAMUEL JOHNSON

Good friendships
are fragile things
and require as much care
as any other fragile
and precious thing.

—RANDOLPH BOURNE

He that walketh
with wise men
shall be wise.

—SOLOMON

I don't care a damn for your loyal service when you think I am right; when I really want it most is when you think I am wrong.

—GENERAL
SIR JOHN MONASH

A wise man
may look ridiculous
in the company of fools.

—THOMAS FULLER

Between friends
there is no need of justice.

—ARISTOTLE

No medicine is more valuable,
none more efficacious, none
better suited to the cure of all
our temporal ills than a friend
to whom we may turn for
consolation in time of trouble,
and with whom we may share
our happiness in time of joy.

—St. Ailred of Rievaulx

Friendship Rules for Your Memory— Remember These

- Your friend's spouse's name
- Your friend's children's names
- Your friend's children's ages
- Your friend's children's hobbies
- Your friend's birthday
- Your friend's anniversary

friendship

The most
exquisite pleasure
is giving pleasure
to others.

—JEAN DE LA BRUYÈRE

It is very easy
to find fault with others
instead of finding out
what the truth is
about them.

—JOHNNY GRUELLE

The Biggest Obstacles
to Friendship

- Shyness
- Fear of rejection
- Fear of intimacy
- Lack of free time
- Not meeting new people

An unshared life
is not living. He who
shares does not lessen,
but greatens, his life.

—STEPHEN S. WISE

Everyone needs help
from everyone.

—BERTOLT BRECHT

Friendship Trivia

Most men and nearly all women report that they would like to have more friends.

Proximity plays a huge role in our choice of friends.

The greatest good
we can do for others
is not to share our riches
but to reveal theirs.

—AUTHOR UNKNOWN

The golden rule
is of no use whatsoever
unless you realize
that it is your move.

—DR. FRANK CRANE

The Most Common Favors Asked for by Friends

Women Ask Women

- Borrow clothes
- Baby-sit
- Give romantic advice
- Play matchmaker
- Loan money
- Borrow jewelry
- Help with a résumé
- Career advice

Men Ask Men

- Help with chores
- Send references

friendship

- Borrow money
  - Stock tips
  - Borrow car
- Play matchmaker
  - Career help
- Get tickets to an important event

Major Friendship
Stress Points

• One friend gets married, the other is single

• One friend has a baby, the other is childless

• One friend has a significant other, the other is dateless

• One friend gets a promotion, the other hates his job

• One friend becomes financially secure, the other
struggles to make ends meet

• One friend becomes gravely ill, the other friend
becomes afraid of losing her

• One friend becomes very busy, the other has too much
time on his hands

friendship

Be charitable and indulgent
to everyone but thyself.

—JOSEPH JAUBERT

Every time we make
a new friend, it is just like
planting another flower
in a beautiful garden
filled with the flowers
of friendship.

—JOHNNY GRUELLE

Thoughts for Success

Study the behavior of the most socially successful person you know and mimic her behavior to have more friends.

Ask your closest friends for feedback on the type of friend you are and learn from their comments.

Work on your marriage to turn your mate into your best buddy.

Keep in mind that the easiest way to get people to like you is to like them.

Make a commitment to yourself not to let any fears hold you back from having the social life you want.

Have more than thou showest;
Speak less than thou knowest.

—WILLIAM SHAKESPEARE

Always be a little kinder
than necessary.

—AUTHOR UNKNOWN

Real unselfishness
consists in sharing
the interests of others.

—GEORGE SANTAYANA

Affirmations for Drawing Wonderful Friends to You

- People of quality are drawn to me

- My friends are people of character and love

- I radiate love, warmth, and joy to others

- I am friends with many wonderful people of all types

- I make new friends wherever I go

- I choose my friends wisely

- God is blessing me with more friends all the time

- I know that I deserve to have quality friendships in my life

- I am open to making new friends

- Many new and wonderful friends are entering my life now

- I am the type of person whom people want to have for one of their closest friends

I am a lovable person.
I have the right to say "no"
to people without losing
their love.

—LEONARD ORR

Be prepared to appreciate
what you meet.

—FRANK HERBERT

When you live
in constant communication
with God, you cannot
be lonely.

—PEACE PILGRIM

Kindness is the language
which the deaf can hear
and the blind can see.

—MARK TWAIN

Rules of Friendship
for Children as Well
as Adults

- Help each other whenever you can

- Don't exclude anyone

- Play fair—play nicely

- Remember to share

- No hitting

- Take turns

- No yelling

- Say "please" and "thank you"

- Be on time

- Say "I'm sorry" when you hurt someone's feelings

- Stay out of trouble

- Mind your manners

friendship

- No name-calling
- Tell the truth
- Be kind
- Try to get along
- Be yourself
- Have fun
- Be extra nice to the shyest, youngest, and oldest one

Strangers are just friends
you haven't met yet.

—AUTHOR UNKNOWN

If you can't say
something nice,
don't say nothin' at all.

—THUMPER, IN *BAMBI*

People change
and forget to tell each other.

—LILLIAN HELLMAN

Forgiveness is the
fragrance of the violet
that clings fast to the heel
that crushed it.

—GEORGE ROEMISCH

How other people are treating us is a mirror for how we're treating ourselves. When we are disregarding our own feelings, we're going to get disregarded on the outside. When we're truly loving and respecting ourselves, that's what we are going to get mirrored back.

—MARGARET PAUL

Easy Ways for Stay-at-Home Moms to Make New Friends

- Go on-line
- Check to see if there are other new moms in your neighborhood
- Join a moms' support group
- Take a parenting class
- Mingle with other new moms at parent/child functions
- Form your own play group
- Join a mothers' group at your church or synagogue

Friendship Trivia

Most women say their friendships are
based on the sharing of feelings and experiences,
while men say that their friendships are
based on shared activities.

Seldom can a heart be lonely,
If it seeks a lonelier still;
Self forgetting, seeking only,
Emptier cups of love to fill.

—FRANCES RIDLEY HAVERGAL

One of the things
I keep learning is that
the secret of being happy
is doing things for
other people.

—DICK GREGORY

The most satisfying thing
in life is to have been
able to give a large part
of oneself to others.

—PIERRE TEILHARD DE CHARDIN

Take a Friend Inventory and List the Different Types of Friends That You Have

- Neighborhood pals
- Work-related buddies
- School chums
- Long-distance relationships
- Mentors and role models
- Family friends
- Friends from your church or synagogue
- Hobby-related chums
- Your children's friends' parents
- Significant-other-related friends

Now study the list and see where most of your friendships are located. Do you need to make any changes?

Let him have the key
of thy heart, who hath
the lock of his own.

—Sir Thomas Browne

The entire sum of existence
is the magic of
being needed by
just one person.

—Vi Putnam

Make one person happy each day and in forty years you will have made 14,600 human beings happy for a little time, at least.

—CHARLEY WILLEY

Manners are like zero
in arithmetic. They may not
be much in themselves,
but they are capable of
adding a great deal of
value to everything else.

—FREYA STARK

Do not use a hatchet
to remove a fly
from your friend's forehead.

—CHINESE PROVERB

Friendship Trivia

Research shows that people
with a wide circle of friends
have fewer illnesses. Get social!

The Truth About Friendship and Money

- Beware of loaning money. Only loan money if you can afford not to have it returned.
- Be considerate of your pal's budget when planning joint activities.
- Refrain from giving any expensive gift that would make your friend feel uncomfortable or indebted to you.
- Keep in mind that everyone spends money differently, so don't try to make your friend budget the same way you do.

The Most Common Reasons That Friendships End

- People change and move on to different relationships
- Friends move away
- Friendships fade between coworkers when one friend leaves the workplace
- Shared interests are no longer a drawing card for the pals
- A romance blossoms for one friend and the friends lose touch
- One friend has a baby and her interests and amount of free time changes
- Betrayal or a disagreement

Friendship is always
a sweet responsibility,
never an opportunity.

—KAHLIL GIBRAN

A friend is, as it were,
a second self.

—CICERO

The Times When Women Said That They Had the Hardest Times Keeping Up with Their Friends

- After a move
- After they have had their first child
- When they get older and become less mobile
- After getting married

The Times When Men Said That They Had the Hardest Times Keeping Up with Their Friends

- After getting married
- After a big promotion
- After each child was born
- During a serious illness

Friendship without
self-interest is one of
the rare and beautiful
things of life.

—JAMES FRANCIS BYRNES

Don't ask of your friends
what you yourself can do.

—QUINTUS ENNIUS

Wishing to be friends is
quick work, but friendship
is a slow ripening fruit.

—ARISTOTLE

Friendship ought to be
a gratuitous joy, like the
joys afforded by art.

—SIMONE WEIL

I want no men around me
who have not the knack
of making friends.

—Frank A. Vanderlip

A friend is never known
till a man has need.

—Author unknown

Friendship may
sometimes step
a few paces
in advance of truth.

—Walter Savage Landor

When good cheer
is lacking, our friends
will go packing.

—Author unknown

How to Be a Really Good Conversationalist

• Put the focus on the other person
and off yourself

• Wear a conversation piece to get the ball rolling

• Be a good listener

• Find out about the person beforehand from
mutual friends

• Have a collection of good opening lines
in your repertoire

• If things are really dull, say something outrageous

• Ask questions

• Cultivate many interests that you can easily talk about

True Friendship

- Develops over time
- Meets both friends' needs and expectations
- Feels good to your emotional side
- Makes sense to your logical side
- Brings you much more joy than sorrow
- Is there in good and bad times

friendship

By associating with good and
evil persons a man acquires the
virtues and vices which they
possess, even as the wind
blowing over different places
takes along good and bad odors.

—THE PANCHATANTRA

The Most Popular Reasons Why Neighbors Make Good Friends

- Common ground and interests
- They can be quite helpful in times of need
- Birds-of-a-feather syndrome
- You see each other regularly and build a sense of familiarity

It is good to give
when asked, but it is better
to give unasked,
through understanding.

—Kahlil Gibran

Gentle ladies,
you will remember
till old age what we did
together in our
brilliant youth.

—Sappho

How to Make Others Feel Good

- Use their help and suggestions
- Ask for their advice
- Point out their positive attributes
- Thank them for their input, favors, and time
- Acknowledge their successes
- Help them reach their goals
- Be fun to be around

friendship

What People Expect from Their Best Friends

- A person to care about them
- Someone to stand by them in good and bad times
- A person who accepts them for who they are
- A person to care for
- Someone to bring enjoyment into their world

Reasons That Dogs
Make Great Pals

- They are loyal

- They love to have fun

- They know how to keep a secret

- They enjoy many different kinds of activities

- They are fun buddies to exercise with

- They are affectionate

- They don't hold grudges

- They are great protectors

- Studies show that petting a dog can actually
  decrease your blood pressure level

- They are wonderful in helping you to meet other people

To my readers who are cat lovers: I didn't include a section on cats as friends, not because they aren't good buddies, but because I am terribly allergic to them and I don't have any firsthand knowledge of their friendships. Sorry!

Friendship Prayer

Dear God,

Please help me to be the one who will bring joy, love, light, and laughter into my friends' lives today. Help me to look past their imperfections and encourage them to follow their dreams. Remind me to be honest and loyal to them at all times. Turn me into the friend that you want me to be. Help me to gladly share in my good fortunes and to rejoice with them in theirs. Please comfort us all in the storms of life and when my life is over, let my friends' lives have been better for my having been a part of theirs. Thank you for the wonderful gift of friendship. Please always bless my friends in all ways.

Amen.

He who looks for
the advantage out of
friendship strips it of
all its nobility.

—Lucius Annaeus Seneca

Friendship is almost always
the union of a part of
one mind with a part
of another; people are
friends in spots.

—George Santayana

There is a magnet in your heart that will attract true friends. That magnet is unselfishness, thinking of others first . . . when you learn to live for others, they will live for you.

—PARAMAHANSA YOGANANDA

For every speck
of fun you give another,
you receive an echo
of that fun yourself.

—JOHNNY GRUELLE

Friends come and go,
enemies linger.

—AUTHOR UNKNOWN

Scatter seeds of kindness everywhere you go;

Scatter bits of courtesy, watch them grow and grow.

Gather buds of friendship, keep them till full-blown;

You will find more happiness than you have ever known.

—AMY R. RAABE

Qualities That Teenage Females Look for in Their Friends

- Shared interests
- Companionship
- Popularity and style
- Ability to keep secrets
- Shared values

friendship

Qualities That Women in Their Twenties Look for in Their Friends

- Common goals
- Networking opportunities
- Love-life advice
- Acceptance
- Shared interests

Qualities That Women in Their Thirties Look for in Their Friends

- Emotional support
- Shared activities
- Fun and companionship
- Parenting and career advice
- Trustworthiness

Qualities That Women in Their Forties Look for in Their Friends

- Warmth
- Shared histories
- Encouragement
- Shared religious beliefs
- Positive attitudes

Qualities That Women in Their Fifties Look for in Their Friends

- Caring
- Time to spend together
- Shared activities
- True friendship
- Sense of humor

Qualities That Women in Their Sixties Look for in Their Friends

- Health advice

- Generosity

- Positive thinking

- Sense of commitment to the friendship

- Shared interests

Qualities That Women in Their Golden Years Look for in Their Friends

- Travel companion
- Positive spirit
- Someone to help out in difficult times
- Encouragement
- Personal satisfaction with life in general

friendship

The friendships which last
are those wherein
each friend respects
the other's dignity to the
point of not really
wanting anything from him.

—CYRIL CONNOLLY

Friendship is neither
a formality nor a mode;
it is rather a life.

—DAVID GRAYSON

I desire to conduct the affairs
of this administration that if at
the end . . . I have lost every
other friend on earth, I shall at
least have one friend left, and
that friend shall be down inside
of me.

—ABRAHAM LINCOLN

Blessed are they who have the gift of making friends, for it is one of God's best gifts. It involves many things, but above all, the power of getting out of one's self, and appreciating whatever is noble and loving in another.

—THOMAS HUGHES

As in the case of wines
that improve with age,
the oldest friendships ought to
be the most delightful.

—CICERO

When to End a Friendship

- You make all of the effort
- You have been betrayed or badly hurt more than once
- Your times together feel like a competition
- You don't really look forward to your times spent together any longer
- Your friend doesn't treat you well
- You no longer have common interests
- Your friend has become a user
- The friendship is physically harmful
- The friendship is emotionally draining
- In your heart of hearts, you want out

I don't know what your destiny will be, but one thing I know: the only ones among you who will be really happy are those who will have sought and found out how to serve.

—ALBERT SCHWEITZER

friendship

Remember the Spiritual Side of Friendship

- Pray for your friends
- Ask your friends to pray for you
- Pray together
- Attend worship services together
- Share your beliefs, even if they are different

My friends have made the story of my life. In a thousand ways they have turned my limitations into beautiful privileges, and enabled me to walk serene and happy in the shadow cast by my deprivation.

—HELEN KELLER

Ways to Have
Especially Good Times
with Your Friends

• Ask your friends what they want to do for a change

• Read your city magazines and newspapers for
special events that will be coming to your area
and make plans to attend

• Become a gracious entertainer

• Go to places you have never been before

• Act like tourists in your own town

• Get outdoors in the fresh air

• Bring along your four-legged buddies

• Spend time with other friends

• Spend time with each other's families

It always fills us
with happiness when we
know we are truly loved
by one we dearly love.

—JOHNNY GRUELLE

One is taught by experience
to put a premium on those
few people who
can appreciate you
for what you are.

—GAIL GODWIN

Are You Suffering from Best-Friend Burnout?

- Do you see each other less often?
- Is she no longer on your speed dial?
- Is she no longer the first friend that you call with good news?
- Are you bored with each other?
- Is she no longer the person you go to for comfort?
- Do you feel that you have outgrown each other?

Good company and
good discourse are the
very sinews of virtue.

—Izaak Walton

Happiness is the
cheapest thing in the world
when we buy it
for someone else.

—Paul Flemming

What Is Your Friendship Style?

• Are you a high- or low-maintenance buddy?

• Do you expect others to call you first?

• Do you expect others to handle all of the social plans?

• Do you expect to always be included in
your friend's social plans?

• Do you expect a lot from your friends emotionally,
financially, or socially?

Ways That Women Say Their Friendships Are Better Than Men's

• More feelings are shared between friends

• More secrets are shared

Ways That Men Say Their Friendships Are Better Than Women's

- Less snits
- More varied activities

What to Do When
You Can't Work Out a
Problem with a Friend

- Agree to disagree

- Turn the other cheek

- Ask another friend to step in and negotiate
for the two of you

- Try to see your friend's point of view

- Put the troubling issue on the back burner
for at least a week

- Write a letter to each other expressing your
different points of view

- Seek professional help if you can't get past it and it
is destroying a friendship that is very important to you

- Remember that people are more important than things

- Take a little time off from each other to cool off

Friendship makes prosperity more brilliant, and lightens adversity by dividing and sharing it.

—CICERO

There are moments in life
when all that we can bear is the
sense that our friend is near us;
our wounds would wince at
consoling words that would
reveal the depths of our pain.

—HONORÉ DE BALZAC

Friendship was given
by nature to be an
assistant to virtue, not a
companion in vice.

—CICERO

The secret of success
in society is a certain
heartiness and sympathy.

—RALPH WALDO EMERSON

Questions to Help You Examine Your Current Friendships

Go through the questions with one friend in mind and then continue on with each of your friends to determine the quality of your friendships.

- Are you compatible in many ways?
- Are you at ease in each other's company?
- Do you ever have to watch what you say? If so, why is that?
- Do you both have the same expectations for the friendship? What are they?
- Do you truly care about each other?
- Are you both equally committed to the friendship?
- Do you take each other for granted?

- Do you have a lot in common?

- How does this friendship compare to
  your other friendships?

- Do you feel safe with this friend emotionally
  and physically?

- How do you handle your differences?

- Does your friend always support you?

- Does your friend look after your best interests?

- Does this friendship allow you to grow?

- Why are you friends?

- Do you feel secure in this relationship?

- How often do you get together?

- How well do you know each other?

- Why do you want to be friends with each other?

- Does she expect too much from you?

- Do you avoid certain topics? If so, why?

- Can you freely express your opinions?

- Can you ask for help without feeling anxious?

- Do you like yourself more or less in her company?
- Do you bring out the best or worst in each other?
- Do you have fun together?
- Are you jealous of each other's successes?
- Do you want to be friends five, ten, or twenty years from now? Do you think that you will be?
- Do you want the best for her?
- Who does your friend remind you of?
- What is your friendship based upon?
- Are you proud to call this person your friend?
- Do you genuinely like this person that you call your friend?
- If you were grading this friendship, what grade would you give it and why?
- What do your other friends think of your friend?
- Is your friend a good influence on you?

friendship

A man cannot
be said to succeed
in this life
who does not satisfy
one friend.

—HENRY DAVID THOREAU

There are only two people
who can tell you the truth about
yourself—an enemy who has
lost his temper and a friend
who loves you dearly.

— ANTISTHENES

friendship

Keep the other person's
well-being in mind
when you feel an attack
of soul-purging truth
coming on.

—BETTY WHITE

The shifts of fortune
test the reliability of friends.

—CICERO

In poverty and
other misfortunes of life,
true friends are
a sure refuge.

—ARISTOTLE

It is better to weep
with wise men
than to laugh with fools.

—SPANISH PROVERB

Friendship that flames
goes out in a flash.

—THOMAS FULLER

Friendship is an art,
and very few persons
are born with a
natural gift for it.

—KATHLEEN NORRIS

Times When Women Say They Need Their Friends the Most

- After a romantic breakup
- During a difficult romance
- After their first child is born
- When a parent dies
- When their self-esteem is low

friendship

Times When Men Say They Need Their Friends the Most

- After getting fired
- After losing a lot of money
- After a romantic breakup
- When a parent dies
- When working for a difficult boss

Every man passes
his life in the search
after friendship.

—RALPH WALDO EMERSON

Forget your woes
when you see your friend.

—PRISCIAN

There is nothing like to see so much as the gleam of pleasure in another person's eye when he feels that we have sympathized with him, understood him, interested ourself in his welfare. At these moments something fine and spiritual passes between two friends. These moments are the moments worth living.

—DON MARQUIS

It is great to have friends when one is young, but indeed it is still more so when you are getting old. When we are young, friends are, like everything else, a matter of course. In the old days we know what it means to have them.

—EDVARD GRIEG

Friends are relatives
you make for yourself.

—EUSTACHE DESCHAMPS

It is the friends you can
call up at 4 A.M. that matter.

—MARLENE DIETRICH

The Ten Fundamental
Rules of Friendship

- Always be a true friend to *yourself*

- Make time for your friends and their needs

- Support your friends and their dreams

- Make yourself enjoyable to be around no matter
what the circumstances are in your life

- Always be on time

- Forgive and forget your friend's mistakes

- Don't expect your friend to meet all of your emotional
needs—you will take care of those on your own

- Take the time needed to develop quality friendships

- Don't judge your friends or criticize them

- Choose your friends very carefully because their
personality traits will rub off on you

friendship

The best rule of friendship
is to keep your heart
a little softer than
your head.

—AUTHOR UNKNOWN

Friendship requires
great communication.

—ST. FRANCIS DE SALES

Friendship is a strong
and habitual inclination
in two persons to promote
the good and happiness
of one another.

—EUSTACE BUDGELL

Greater love hath no man
than this, that a man lay
down his life for his friends.

—JOHN 15:13

How to Be
Your Own
Best Friend

• Put your needs up high on your list of priorities

• Follow your heart

• Get to know and love your true self

• Regularly make time to be alone

• Stop the voice of inner criticism

• Choose your mate and friends carefully

• Every day do something just for you

• Eat right

• Never stop learning

• Exercise

• Work on improving your life

• Keep growing

- Set goals and go after them
- Ask for help whenever you need it
- Have an excellent role model or mentor
- Have a spiritual foundation for your life

Seek those who find your road agreeable, your personality and mind stimulating, your philosophy acceptable, and your experiences helpful. Let those who do not, seek their own kind.

—JEAN-HENRI FABRE

The only way
to have a friend
is to be one.

—RALPH WALDO EMERSON

Make a List of Ten Things That You Can Do to Improve Your Friendships

1.

2.

3.

4.

5.

6.

7.

8.

9.

10.

Make a List of the Main Qualities
That You Want in Your Friends

1.

2.

3.

4.

5.

6.

7.

8.

9.

10.

friendship

Make a List of the Qualities
That Make You a Good Friend

1.

2.

3.

4.

5.

6.

7.

8.

9.

10.

Write Down the Names of the Eight Best Friends You've Made During Your Lifetime

1.

2.

3.

4.

5.

6.

7.

8.

*Consider writing each of these wonderful friends a letter
and sharing your feelings with them.*

Write Down the Five Happiest Times You've Spent with Your Friends

1.

2.

3.

4.

5.

Can these times be re-created? What can you learn from these memories to help you improve the times you spend with your friends nowadays?

ABOUT THE AUTHOR

Cyndi Haynes is a best-selling author of seven books in the 2,002 series, including *2,002 Ways to Show Your Kids You Love Them* and *2,002 Ways to Cheer Yourself Up.* Her books have been published in twelve languages. To promote her books she has appeared on hundreds of radio and television programs, including *Ricki Lake* and *Gordon Elliott.* Her books have been written about in numerous publications, including *Glamour, Redbook,* and *Cosmopolitan.* She lives in Indiana with her husband, son, two golden retrievers, and a Bernese mountain dog.